A COLLECTION OF WILDFLOWERS

CHARLY WHITE

A COLLECTION OF WILDFLOWERS

CHARLY WHITE

palavro
PUBLISHING

A Collection of Wildflowers

By Charly White

© Charly White

ISBN: 9781912092291

First published 2024

Published by Palavro, an imprint of
the Arkbound Foundation (Publishers)

Arkbound is a social enterprise that aims to promote social inclusion, community development and artistic talent. It sponsors publications by disadvantaged authors and covers issues that engage wider social concerns. Arkbound fully embraces sustainability and environmental protection. It endeavours to use material that is renewable, recyclable or sourced from sustainable forest.

Arkbound
Rogart Street Campus
4 Rogart Street
Glasgow, G40 2AA

www.arkbound.com

Supporters

The publication of this book was enabled through a dedicated crowdfunding campaign on Crowdbound.org. Among the many supporters, we are particularly grateful to:-

Daniel White

Jennifer White

Phillip White

Mary McColley

Ayman Chafai

Kayley Phillips

Dafydd Podmore

Taslima Alam

Stephen Israel

To my brother, Danny.

Can I Have This Dance?

I am composing a song
that will encourage me
to move through this world
with softness, ease and grace

I hope you will join me
in this dance

...

WILDFLOWERS

*

A randomly collected, colourful pocket of nature.

Unique to each person's findings, tastes and adventures.

Completely imperfect.

Beautiful.

*

Capturing Beauty

I am capturing words
moments and images
that I find beautiful
in the hopes
that someone else
sees beauty
through the same lens

Collage

Everyone has
an eye
for beauty

our lenses may differ
shutters may blink

at varying
moments

allowing us to capture
an optimum of wonders
colours and tales

all angled
differently

to complement
the entirety

of this breathtaking

work of art

The Wild In Us

How do we see
the beauty
in wildflowers

yet harness
the beauty
in our
wild selves

DAISY

*

A connection to the magic in our lives.

A rediscovery of our inner child.

If we tied together our youthful wonder and adult wisdom,

how powerfully joyful we could be

*

Blind Trust

Leap

with an open heart and

trust

that the world will

catch you.

A Gift From Nature

Endless wonder
fearless curiosity
wildflowers collected from dirt

tied together
with hopeful intent

to keep my heart and soul a child
to keep my life
uniquely wild

Questions

What did your heart dream of as a child?

When did it change?

Why did it change?

Who made it change?

Why did you let them?

A Gift In A Question

I was asked

'What is the most beautiful thing you've seen today?'

and as I pondered on the wonders
that had graced my way
I wished
I was asked this
everyday

Set Yourself Free

Find what makes your heart smile
what gets your hands dirty
with glittering mud
collected from your childhood
with a fierce rebellion against
being stored away

forgotten

This jar contains
your purest self
your wildest soul
your fearlessly ambitious
hopes and dreams
your shameless self-belief

It is far too precious
to be stored away

forgotten

Ensemble

Familiar stranger
singing
in a *langue étranger*
a fairy-lit room
powered by music
and applause
eyes of awe
smiles of *gentillesse*
words of encouragement
hidden talent
reserved
for this moment
a moment
I could live in
toujours

Skipping To The Same Beat

It wasn't until I met you
that I truly understood
the depths of a person
beyond their form
the hypnotising powers of
a smile, a laugh, a kind heart

transparent and pure

I feel my soul
being drawn to yours
through songs, stories
and future dreams

endless allure

two starkly different beings
somehow, finding themselves
on the same path

what a wonderful stroke
of dumb luck

Signs

We turn to the stars
and shapes in the clouds
desperately seeking a sign
instead
of asking our heart
what it truly desires

have we really
more trust
in the clouds
than in
our own hearts
?

Making Rainbows

We hold our emotions
like dark clouds
collecting each droplet
until we're destined

TO BURST

an explosive release of thunder
a beautifully harsh spell of snow
a simple light shower of sadness

exactly what we need
to allow our

clear blue minds

to grace
the light
of day
again

Silly Sock

Sometimes
a simple dropped sock
on the ground
will make your eyes flood
with tears

It's okay

let your emotions
find their release

the only thing silly
is the bright blue duck
painted upon your sock

It's okay

it will find its way
back to its proper place

and so will you

Identity

A few letters
strung together
a look, a style
the way I walk
what makes me, me?

the words of others?
a reputation?
the regard of you
or me?

the things I own?
the place I'm from?
the language that I speak?

something I can choose and change
or pre-determined for me?

So bizarre to even question this
the answer clear to see:

the one and only with rights
to this body and mind
is certainly me

Voilà who creates the formula
to determine who I feel to be

If unsatisfied, displeased, unaccepted at all
you can take that up with
(not) me.

Dangerous Expectations

What do I want from life?

my own answer
will be
the root
of all
my disappointment
and failures

unless I say, simply

to be happy
despite it all

_____ Of The Unknown

Why do we associate the unknown
with fear?

Automatically programmed
to predict the worst
filling our crystal balls
with darkness and dread
change = bad
let me cocoon myself
in my homemade patchwork blanket
and hide from this cold wind

But what if
this wind were to lift you
gently
to new horizons?
unveil hidden wonders
landscapes, cultures
people, places, ideas
b e a u t y

What if
you channelled this fear
into excitement and curiosity

filling your crystal ball
with lightness and hope

Would you get out of bed?

To Be Truly Rich

I want to be rich
with time
memories
and happiness

money
has no
meaning
beyond
survival

Older and Wiser

We spend our whole lives
never fully embracing

where we are

we spend our youth
wishing to be older, wiser

yet when gifted with time

we spend our old age
wishing to be young again

how sad
we did not grow
to see

the wise people
that we aspired
to be

Little Nows

Life is made up
of little nows
distracting us with
the whys and hows

where meaning is sought
with purpose in hand
desperately seeking
with heads in the sand

predicting and plotting
for our future selves
our current needs packed-up
and put on the shelf

forgetting, neglecting,
failing to see how
our life is made up of those
little nows

25

25 years
of learning who I am
and who I want to be

25 years
of making mistakes
and accepting failures

25 years
of making friends
and losing strangers

25 years
of searching for my path
and getting lost

25 years
of wishful thinking, empty dreams
and dumb luck

25 years
of living

Morning Sky

Hues of orange
pink and red
merge together

offering their beauty and warmth
to the clear blue canvas
that is their stage

performing a most eloquent
and graceful dance
that will never be seen
in the same way again

a one-time show
each critic
will remark
differently

a choice:
to notice the imperfection
to appreciate the exclusivity
to capture the potential

to be inspired

I Surrender

Instead of
crushing my mind
under the
unbearable pressure
of fulfilment and success

I choose to surrender

and allow
the current
to guide
my uncertain
path with
excitement
fear
acceptance
and trust

Another Daisy On The Chain

Another year gifted with
the luxury of time
another jar of memories
I get to label mine

Another year of lessons learnt
challenges and trials
a blank canvas, splattered with
hopes and tears and smiles

Another year of cherished moments
others to erase
more wrinkle, frown and laughter lines
find home upon my face

Another year of precious people
found and held and lost
more days spent seeking sunshine
whilst fighting off the frost

Another year of chances
Another year to try
Another year to spread my wings
Another year to fly

Creating You

What if, today
you existed
as a blank and empty page
perfectly untouched and new
a spotlight on the stage

What colours would you paint you with?
What words would you write you with?
What image would embody you?
What melody would sing your tune?

What if, today
you believed
this creation to be true
you are not pre-determined
there are no fixed-place rules

What if, today
you allowed
this magic to shine through
to be the author
artist, sculptor, director, composer
of you

It Knows Your Potential

The world is
waiting for you
to grab it

to create something
so beautiful

to leave it
in awe

inspiring
forever
more

Expand Your World

Leave, just once

and see where your heart takes you

...

ROSE

*

All of the beauty of falling in love

and all of the pain.

*

Falling

I can feel my heart

f
a
l
l
i
n
g

weakening

with each soft word
and sweet smile
that you offer me

I am sure
I am not ready

but I dare not
resist

U + I

A journey to embark on
together hand in hand
wading through the waters
laying in the sand

Testing all our limits
reaping our rewards
loving with our gentleness
fighting with our swords

A tennis match, a rollercoaster
extremes of high and low
at times you're most beloved
at times become a foe

2 compositions mixing
clashing to create
a messy raw concoction
of something, sometimes great

One could not be without the other
whichever way you try
an essential chemical make-up
of the letters U + I

Longing

I start to feel
that ache to find
the 'other' by my side

the rollercoaster ride: to fall in love
with someone else's body, soul and mind

thoughts, opinions
merge with mine
a tangled mess
of admiration
vulnerability
and fear

Careful What You Wish For

Sometimes, I feel
it's not worth

all of the bad
this magnet attracts

but sometimes
I'm left hungry

craving it
quand même

The Chase

I could see it
in your eyes
smell it
all over you: the lust
for another

but not brave enough, still
to go for your prey
or even
to set my heart free
to the wild

I was strung along

bearing the pain of my fate

with a smile, still hoping

you'd change your mind

Distance

I laid my heart out

bare and broken

thinking

I'd convinced you

to stay

...

when simply

I scared you

to wait

until I was

5925 miles

away

...

A Bad Compromise

I so desperately
wanted you
to stay

I was ready
to throw
my life
away

Irrelevant

The thought of you
loving someone else
so much so that

I
become
irrelevant

makes me feel
that maybe

I
already
am

Confidential

I know you are
the only one
I've loved

I've hurt before
but never enough
to cry my heart out
into these pages

Lingering

Why do you still cross my mind?
a thousand times
I've convinced myself
to accept
our not meant to be, happily never after
I've grown
I've changed
I've flourished
without you
with the biggest help from your absence
but still
even as the tiniest grain of sand
amongst my desert of thoughts
you're undeniably, happily
and.ever.so.stubbornly.
still here

Familiar Strangers

I often wonder
what it would be like
to meet again

but I'm not sure
we would recognise
each other

I am not
the same me

as our old
and broken 'we'

Hindsight

Only after

breaking free

have I

been able

to see

how toxic

being 'us'

made me

The Making Of Me

I want you
to see
how losing you
has been

The Making Of Me

Naked

I am naked

on these pages

at my most

vulnerable and honest

at my most

fragile and strongest

Love Letter To Paris

Paris, a land *étranger*
displaced and far from home
amidst the life and hustle
still, so easily alone

Such beauty that surrounds me
in elegance and grace
how lucky to be stood within
the magic of this place

Paris, you start to welcome me
a familiarity grows
I begin to find my rhythm here
amidst the highs and lows

The friends who become family
through tough and testing days
rooted with support and love
like knots that fail to fray

Paris, now you excite me
as opportunities stream
and all look on in awe, how great
to be 'living the dream'

Not blind *à l'autre côté*
or struck with naivety
but for now, at least,
I choose to be
embraced in your beauty

Paris, no more étrange to me
we've found our own sweet flow
a sense of home embedded in
this space that's helped me grow

I hope you know my gratitude
when stripped of loyalty
and open arms of welcome if
one day you notice me

Paris, c'est le fin de nous
je voudrais te remercie
jusqu'on se revoir encore un jour
je te garderai au coeur
- Charly

DANDELION

*

Seemingly innocent, even pleasant to the eye

with its pretty form and bright colour.

A weed that is destructive and extremely difficult to remove.

*

Little Ants

I am in awe
of this planet
our people
a society
completely made-up
yet convincingly normal

little ants
scattering around
just trying to survive
some bigger, some smaller,
some richer, some poorer

all concepts
made by man
all violently
carved by hand

composing a symphony
of madness
to which
we all partake
we all abide
we can't comprehend
yet can't subside

Pest Remover

There are trees, older
than I could ever imagine
seeing life, breathing
nourishing the earth
with their wholesome beauty

maybe

our time

here is

cut

so

short

because

instead of

loving the earth

like the trees

we choose

to destroy it

Irony

We look on in awe
at the natural wonders
of this world

flock to witness
the breathtaking beauty:
the oceans, mountains
and gentle giants, at peace
in their natural habitats

whilst simultaneously
exploiting them
for our own
convenience

and doing nothing
at all
to save them

Natural Beauty

Why do we see more beauty in
our constructed 'natural' parks
than in muddied ponds, filled with life
a single, thriving, lily pad

if we approached each
with the same respect
without 'don't litter' and 'keep off' signs
maybe we'd see
a cleaner tomorrow

prospering
with love
and real beauty

Happy And Kind

If our motive is not
to be happy and kind
let us take a step back
and question our minds

Let's care more about giving
even when we get less
than constantly wanting
more things to impress

Let's care more about sheltering
our friends on the street
than aspiring to be more like
the rich and elite

Let's care more about humans
getting their rights
than choosing convenience
ignoring their plights

Let's care more about selflessness
and sharing to those
who are silently suffering
on our front doors

Let's care more about spreading
our resources and powers
than hoarding each luxury
convinced that it's 'ours'

Let's care more about protecting
the earth and its health
than failing to consider
anything but ourselves

Let's care more about everyone
living together
as the parts of our whole
are as crucial as ever

Let's care more about changing
our motives and minds
let's prioritise living
Happy and Kind

Simple Cosy Lives

With injustice, strife and endless plight
I feel too small to take this fight
what can I do? but carry on
with my simple, cosy life

Then power grows, a silent kite
drifting closer to my home
its edges sharp, prepared to strike
the simple, cosy life I've known

I shout and warn of danger!
how we must defend our rights!
but not yet feeling threatened
my friends turn out their lights

With injustice, strife and endless plight
we feel too small to take this fight
what can we do? but carry on
with our simple, cosy lives

Illogical Battle Ground

I am embarrassed
of my privilege
that removes my target
from the firing-line

it is a luxury
I have not earned

Programmed Not To Care

Why are we so quick
to conform, obey and trust
those with our worst intentions
at heart?

submitting to
our rigid patterns that
train us into
thoughtless machines

switching compassion
for efficiency
forgetting our humanity

Are we too scared to break the rules?
too awkward to bend them?
too stuck in our ways
to reconnect and reboot?

Or do we really just trust
the man in the suit
with our worst intentions
at heart?

Competitive Salary - Apply Now!

Instead of stocks and sales
and marketing techniques

let's strive to be the best

the most innovative and creative

the most successful

in restoring our compassion
and bettering the world

You Need To Be Ambitious

Why is someone with
'high ambition'

the person
chasing a corporate career

not the person
creating a kinder world

?

Where We've Gone Wrong

On our one precious journey
in what we call life
we learn how to prosper
and hide from the strife

In search for a meaning
convinced there's a way
a right destination
to find which, we pray

Caught up in the chaos
of what we should do
forgetting our nature
and how to be true

Rationing all of our trust
and our care
not wanting to listen
not willing to share

Our modern day screens
display 'Try Again'
our search results empty -
try asking a friend

In our wealth of discoveries
we wish we'd have known
that our one precious journey
would be wasted, alone

Plagiarism

How do I unravel
the mess
that has been left
in my mind

through deceit
bad habits
bad influences
and lies

social constructs
that did not
ask permission
to ruin

the pure
blank canvas
that was mine

The Power Of Choice

Strip me of my fun
bleed the enjoyment from my life
go ahead - *allez-y*
you have my permission, authority

I need you, you see
so do what you must
leave me lingering behind
with lust, in trust
that you're the best for me

I can't do better
can't afford to take the risk
so keep me here, prisoner
in this tiny space
safe.comfortable.bound.
by my own
confidence, apprehension and fear.

How lucky I am
with this stability.

How powerful I am
with this choice.

A Genius Idea

I Propose:
we build four concrete walls
to shut us from the outside world
escape the light of day
and all of nature's healing gifts

Let's follow
strict and rigid regimes
that strip us of our freedom

Let's push ourselves
restrict our joys
and give away our time

To make room for
the *really important* stuff

LET'S MAKE MORE MONEY
and spend each day
pretending
that it makes us
happy
...
you in?

What Experience Do You Have?

I spend so much of my life working

for others

for money

for holidays

for status

for reputation

for something to do

for helping out

for the 'experience' that it robs me of

for everyone else

~~for me~~

Pawns

how helpless
to play
the pawn
desperately
hoping that
the world
will choose
to treat you
kindly

Together Stronger

We will say NO
louder and longer
until they take
our right to speak

We will stand tall
bolder and stronger
whilst they try
to make us meek

We won't back down
Determined Soldiers
our rage
making it hard
to see

so much so that
during this process
we've forgotten
who's the enemy

Pretty Paper

How are we so easily fooled
into believing that money
is the key to success
the solution
to our problems

Carelessly, we exchange
our most precious items
just to touch it - blind
to the fact that
this shiny coin of deceit
will only be used
to buy back

Everything
we so
willingly
gave away

Investing Tips

Invest in people
find security in friends
instead of your
unsatisfyingly full
bank account

Thank You, Sir

We sit back and accept
there's simply not enough

as we watch them buy
their cars and yachts

whilst handing us
their penny sweets

that slowly

make us

rot

A Worthy Cause

We challenge our brightest minds
to figure out how
to make the most money
with the incentive
of even more

ignoring
the infinite poverty
outside our minds
outside our doors

there's not enough
capacity for
compassion

inside us
anymore

How Lucky Are You?

We are funding
the lottery

instead of feeding
the hungry

convinced
that the winning hand

is worth more
than our

h u m a n i t y

Who Wants To Be A Millionaire?

Why are people
so proud to say
'I want to be a millionaire'

Is there truly
any satisfaction
to be had
from showing off
your fancy things
to the rest
of the starving
world
?

Contagious

Greed
has become
the most toxic poison
to the human race

it has forced
to extinction
all of our
compassion

Dear Stranger On The Metro

Vulnerable, frustrated, annoyed, upset
it's funny
these emotions feel unworthy
of being
but they are.

A petty theft, pickpocket
but my pocket's a part of my things!

I hate this concept
want nothing to do
with materialism *mais voilà*
c'est là - it's there
and it's mine.

How silly it seems
but this card is me
it's quite literally
my identity

How scary when gone
what proof do I have?
who will believe
just me, my word?

I double pinky swear it's me!
Now let me home to see my family
…
Please

Convicted Thief

I am so consumed
with worry
of losing
my time

I do not notice
my own theft
in broad daylight

The Power Of Resistance

Does resisting

make us

more powerful

for taking

a stand

or weaker

for failing

to accept

and be

at peace

with our

reality

?

Fighting Fire With Fire

The hatred you see
spilling out from this person
consuming them, overbearingly
forcing them to reflect it
onto the rest of the world
has come from
a more powerful source
in too close a vicinity
they couldn't help
but absorb it

maybe
if we starve them
of this hatred

they will feed off
our compassion
instead

Deeply Rooted

Will I ever free myself
from the world's standards
constructs and lies?

If I choose my own narrative today
will the voices of doubt
and judgement of non-conformity
grow back stronger tomorrow?

Like a stubborn weed
deeply rooted
it has been watered
for too long

You didn't think you'd be rid of it so easily?

You need to get your hands dirty
acknowledge all you've given to help it to grow
and the process you need to undergo
to rid your mind of its toxic remains

to create space

for your own beautiful flower

to bloom

FOXGLOVE

*

A poisonous plant with a 'kill or cure' label.

How toxic our minds can be and how strong we need to be

to keep fighting.

*

A Beautiful Mess

Sometimes
my breath
is taken away

by the beauty
that surrounds me

sometimes
by the devastation

what a cruel
messed-up world

that allows
such devastating
beauty

Unwelcome

I feel a
numbness
that is
holding me
prisoner
from living
my life

I don't
know how
it got here

or how
to make it
leave

Overwhelm

I have

so much work

to do

on myself

IDON'TKNOWWHERETOSTART

Practise What You Preach

I have an army
of uplifting
motivational mantras
on my side

yet when life strikes
I crumble
at its mercy

Beautiful Oblivion

I have so much
to learn
from others

admiration
for those
who themselves
are oblivious
to their own
beautiful attributes
that I envy

oblivion can be wonderful
carefree, modest
but so cruel
tricking you
deceiving you

to the point
where you wish away
the root of our envy
that, which makes you

Beautifully Unique

Broken Mirrors

What if we believed
the kind words of strangers

over the sharp
cutting mirrors

that glisten and shine
all the more brightly

each time
they scar us

with their harsh
deformed truths

Pristine Condition

We want to keep everything

Pristine and Perfect

no signs of damage

no signs of life

Fuelling The Fire

I'm sick
of feeding
my bad habits
more than
I feed
myself

My Most Dangerous Friend

I can feel it
surfacing

a darkness

from the pit
of my stomach

a quiet growl
that makes me cave
it's what I crave

My Destructive Companion

growing and
getting stronger

with every
reinforcement
I willingly
feed it

instead of
feeding
myself

Uprooted

Uprooted with
ungentle hands
that care not for
your state of mind
won't fret if you
get left behind

grasping to remains
to intensify the pain
addicted
to your souvenirs
prescribing each
as needed drugs

to keep you
in your
past

rooted
there
f o r e v e r

The Take Down

I feel the battle
commence
between my ego
and my well-being

although I've trained for this
made sure I'm strong
the ego has such wicked tricks
knows to strike
at my weakest
knows the weight
of its words

gently planting its tiny seeds
of destructive thoughts
humming all the while
almost unnoticed

lovingly nourishing them
with water and sunlight

until they're strong enough
confident enough
to take over

Be Careful, Dear

I want to feel
light
to float
to shed
the disgusting weight
my body carries
from this life
and all of the burdens
it lays onto me

I will do
what I can
to keep
light enough
to fly

but I'm scared

the line is
so thin
between this life
and the next

Pause

Time to stop.

pause,

b r e a t h e

the moment I've been waiting for

neglecting the now

to overindulge

in the fantasy

of what's to come

but now

that moment has arrived

I've forgotten

how to live it

the present, a stranger

I'm unsure

how to approach

QUICK!

distract, plot, plan

something new

fall into the safety net

of your overworked, over-active mind

so much to see

predict, pursue, perform

cannot wait

for that

pause,

Olive Pit Of Dread

.

A tiny olive pit
of fear

.

hard to swallow
impossible to digest

.

embedded as deeply
into my conscience

.

there is no way
to safely remove

.

this harmless feeling
of dread

.

planted the moment
I chose this path

.

silently praying
this fear

.

will not
grow into
regret

.

Trust The Timing Of Your Life

To trust the timing
of your life
is the most wonderfully
frustrating thing
holding your hand
whilst simultaneously
casting shadows
of uncertainty and doubt

To close your eyes
and keep walking
requires a courage
hard to maintain
your shadows echoing: *what if*
if only - taunting you
with 'perfect' ideas and possibilities
that were never meant to be

Without which
you may actually be satisfied
with your reality

with the simple trust
in the timing
of your life

Living The Dream

'Living the dream'
whose dream?
is it mine?
sometimes, overwhelmed
sometimes, just fine

I try to be in awe
of the luck I have found
sometimes, just try to get up
from the ground

Lucky? yes
Happy? yes
Always? no

Living the dream?
maybe … sometimes

Things change:
people, moods, seasons,
dreams

I'm Fine

Yes, I'm all good
I'm okay
I'm fine

head up, I go on
nurtured by time

each day a Band-Aid
to smother the wound
naively hoping
all will heal soon

plastering smiles
hiding too well
the pain underneath
so no-one could tell

aware that a simple
word or a thought
can rip them off harshly
deep and cutthroat

so, careful I go on
being hunted by time

Yes, I'm all good
I'm okay
I'm fine

Emotion Cycles

Wake up, smile
a deep breath
of beautiful fresh air
determination in my bones
bird song accompanying
skip in step
wondrous new heights

Wake up drowning. short gasping breaths. not enough air
HEAVINESS IN MY BONES
today the birds cry - please don't ask why. confusion, overwhelm
CRASHING FROM THE SKY

Maybe, if I curl up small
close my eyes for a while
tomorrow, I will again
be fine

Wake up, smile

Hamster Wheel

To realise
that the rest of the world
does not share your pain
cuts the deepest wound
of betrayal

leaving you
hopeless and lonely

wondering how
to jump back
onto the wheel

-RECKLESSLY-FAST-WITHOUT-MERCY-OR-END-

wondering, actually
whether it's worth
getting back on
at all

How Dare They

I am offended
by a world
that keeps moving
amidst my grief

every
tiny
thing
bouldered over
by a devastating weight

into a meaningless
nothing

how dare they complain
how dare they laugh
how dare they sigh and roll their eyes

with their freedom
from this weight

that I would never
wish onto
their shoulders

When Time Stands Still

The clocks keep ticking
the birds keep singing
the sun keeps setting and rising
the world does not
stand still
on your hardest days or
most heartbreaking moments
your devastation
stops
only
you.

You must try
to keep moving
with the rest
of the world
and not
get left

behind

Alive

At last

I can feel

my body

fighting

albeit, struggling

but alive

HYDRANGEA

*

A flower that changes colour depending on its environment.

Teaching us to adapt and overcome challenges, to blossom into change,

to flourish and grow as our own beautiful selves.

*

Shift

Sometimes, all it takes

is one person

one conversation, one

moment

to completely

shift

your perspective of

your world, of

yourself

Holding Myself Back

I have forever
feared decisions
wanting to blame others
for their
bad-calls and misjudgements
instead of allowing myself
to blossom
into
the change

Unqualified

Who are you
to judge
my person?

You have *no idea*
what it took
to become her
or the *wonderful things*
she will do

See With Your Own Eyes

Why have we allowed

someone else

to define

our own perception

of beauty?

Self Destruct

I will not let

anyone's expectations

including my own

destroy

my ability

to be happy

Fool's Trap

To pursue your passion
and make it your profession
your purpose
is a form of pure genius
in the face of those
who tried
to fool us
into leading
a 'proper'
unhappy life

Main Course

We always take most pleasure
from the first and last bite
a fleeting moment of mindful awareness
filling us with content

But what about the middle?
the part that sustains us
leaving us neither too hungry nor full
in a beautifully healthy balance
of nourishment

Let us not
use this template
for the rest of our lives
- forever searching
- for that extra something sweet
and missing out
on a wonderful
main course

Personal Project

I want to work
for myself
on myself
to develop my mind
in my biggest project
titled: Me

To put the time in, needed
to become the best me
within my capacity

Only then
can any other work
I put into the world
be of any
true value

Misconceptions

'someone who takes care of themselves'

Def:
someone who considers
their ~~appearance~~ health
a priority
and cares deeply about
how they ~~look~~ feel

Who's The Fairest Of Them All?

Do you like yourself

when you close your eyes

and all that's left

to judge

is your soul

?

The Creative Type

Convinced I wasn't
'the creative type'

lacking the talent
I needed
to express myself

how sad
how frustrating
how suffocating

how far

from the truth

how DETERMINED I am

to prove myself wrong.

Resilience

We are all resilient
because we are all
still going

Sculpture Of Strength

Live outside your comfort zone
embrace life's challenges
test your limits, allow
the hands of the world
to work freely, moulding
a sculpture
that is strong
weathering inevitable
merciless storms
with your beautifully unique
scars of success

Malleable

I am an
ever-changing
s c u l p t u r e

moulded
by many different
inspiring hands
minds, ideas
and places

I am malleable

and that's
what makes me
strong.

The Climb

An unfaltering perseverance
weathering the fiercest storms
of emotions, fatigue and doubt

Trudging through high grass
and muddied waters, often alone
but determined to plod on

don't turn back
end in sight
one more push
clawing
grasping
fighting
to reach your goal
and place your flag of victory
on top of your most challenging hill

Proudly.

Already

I want to ~~make~~ keep making
myself proud

Relief

The thought
of having kept
everything I believed I wanted:
- the unhealthy relationships
- the destructive patterns of living
- my 'sometimes' happy life
brings a fear
that overwhelms me
with gratitude
and such relief

that I did not get
everything
I ever wanted

Thank You __

The knowledge that my good luck
may never have directed my life
to the journey that I'm on
to become the person that I am
scares me to submission
with a bow of unwavering gratitude
to whoever I should thank
for this undeserved miracle

Becoming Butterflies

Never would I have imagined
my own potential
to grow

*

to transform
into
a butterfly
*

without even realising
I was
the caterpillar

Part Of The Ride

What is life
without joy, love
pain and loss?

I would rather feel each
fiercely

the pure, heart-warming moments
amongst the hardest goodbyes

my emotions carving
the most life-like human sculpture
beautifully messy
and imperfect

proof
I have lived
a meaningful life

Journey To Balance

The journey
to finding balance
is one I'm not sure
I will ever reach the end of
not sure a final destination
really exists
there will forever be imperfections
better paths and wiser decisions
but I will keep trying
to embrace the journey
in all
its messy glory

SUNFLOWER

*

My favourite flower - an explosion of yellow happiness.

Showing us how beautiful life can be when we take care of ourselves

and face the sun.

*

Nourishment

Close your eyes
feel the sun
on your face
there is nothing
quite so powerful
in washing your body
clearing your mind
or soothing your soul

try it
with a smile
soak it all in
savour this feeling
of being
fully
fearlessly
alive

Best Version Of Me

The 'best version' of me
is not me
at my skinniest or prettiest
in my nicest outfit or
most flattering angle

But is me on the days
I choose to speak kindly
to myself
and let that kindness
b l o s s o m

The Magic Of Mindfulness

The moments
I am mindful
are the moments
I am most happy
with the world
with myself

Proof We Are Whole

the woman dining alone
the flowers you buy for yourself
the strangers that make you smile
the pen that holds your hand
the book that sends you gently to sleep
the songs that open their arms, without judgement
the films you lay your emotions upon
the warm drink that shoulders the cold
the stupidity of life that draws laughter from your belly
the time you have without searching for another
the love that surrounds you

even whilst alone

Gift Of Solitude

Being alone
can be such
a revitalising gift
I'm unsure why
it scares us
so much
are you really
so undeserving
of your
own
magical
company?

Self-Love

Take care
of your sweet body
nourish it
with the freshest air
and clearest water
wrap your arms
around your back
and bask
in your own
embrace

the only thing
strong enough
to truly
heal your soul

is you

It Knows Best

Listen to your body
more than anything else
- any book
- any expert
- any person
who is not precisely you

It knows
what it needs

It knows
what is best

It knows
the way

Simple Admiration

I idolise the sunflowers
for their unfaltering conviction
in facing the sun
determined to find
whatever allows them
to smile
to flourish
to grow

how I admire
this simply beautiful
approach to life
and aspire
to live
the same way

Yellow Sponge

Today, I am grateful
for the thoughtfulness of others
expressed in their own
unique and beautiful ways

Today, I am lucky
to be on the receiving end
of the world's kindness

to be able
to absorb it all
like a yellow sponge
watered with happiness
full of love
reluctant
to let go
of
a
single
drop

.

To Live In Awe

Awe is such a wonderful thing
to experience
to attract
to find
I seek it out
as often as I can
welcoming it
with warmth
making my admiration
so blatantly obvious
that its ego will take note

silently acknowledging
my desperate plea
to keep gracing my life
with its wondrous beauty

I will chase you forever,
unashamedly

Chasing The Sun

We are all sunflowers

chasing the sun

but it's never

in the same place

at the same time

for us all

Happy Place

Whenever I find

* a happy place *

I close my eyes
and feel the moment
so that whenever I face
the darkness again
my mind
will carry me

* there *

without
a trace

DAFFODIL

*

The flower that will always remind me of home.

A nostalgic glow of warmth and joy.

The feeling of being surrounded by bright yellow buds and people you love.

*

Noun: Home

The definition of home
is not to be found
in a dictionary

but within
your heart.

The Valleys

The accent that sings
your favourite song
hugs you
from behind
to warm you
in its welcoming embrace
rolling from your tongue
as a secret whisper
that others can't understand

The Land of Song
whose lyrics fill my heart
with pride
a smile to pass along
whilst savouring
that sweet, sweet scent
of home

Our Tree

A family tree
with roots
deeply embedded
in Welsh soil
singing with the winds
withstanding the elements
with pride
each branch: a complement
a tale
a legacy
a support
a connection
that brings together
each unique energy
to form one
strong
beautiful creation
standing tall
upon the hill

Fy Mrawd

My protector
(against all bad and scary things)

My personal body guard
(against all bad and scary people)

My company
(amidst all lonely, scary nights)

My reassurance
(amidst failures and uncertain times)

My first ever friend

My partner in crime

My brother

Motherly Instinct

The mother with her arm
around her child
a simple display
of comfort
protection
and love

how our bodies
speak so much louder
than our words
without
even
trying

Graduation

A smile you can't control or hide
sometimes graced with tears
taking front to throw aside
all self-doubt and fears

A much well-earned acknowledgement
that rallies in a crowd
of beaming faces, showing-off
how much we're all so proud

The Welsh-est Home In Canada

Daffodils,
gracefully graffitied
where space can be found
next to Welsh Dragons
subtle and proud

Foundations made up
from a land far away
scattering memories
of such special days

Laughter and happiness
precious to see
wrapped up in love
shared between family

Kept extra close
to make a new start
in a beautiful home
with Wales, at its heart

- for Margaret

My Brother

A light
that has forever gifted me
with guidance, support and belief
helping to shape
my proudest qualities
the strongest elements
of my character and mind

a torch amidst fear
a candle amidst chaos
sunshine amidst the gloomiest days
a map
a teacher
a voice of reason
my weirdest, most annoying friend

without whom
my world
would never be
as bright

My Tribe

Sometimes
life brings you to your people
your souls connect
instantly, silently acknowledging
that once upon a time
this would have been your tribe

Sometimes
life offers a journey
to embark upon together

Sometimes
just a fleeting *rencontre*
leaving you enlightened
yet despaired
filling your emptiness with hope
that your paths will cross again

some time

A Happy Home

There are times
when I am
so pleasantly surprised
by how beautiful
my world is
and I thank my mind
for giving me
such a wonderful place
to live

Free Souls

When your soul was freed and scattered
through the mountains and the trees
my soul, too, broke to pieces
to join you in the breeze

And so I make my journey
my heart sets out to roam
to find you strong and clear
in each beloved place we know

And foreign lands
you never had the chance to go and see
no longer bound by life's limits
your soul is truly free

Leaving me a puzzle
pieces of you to be found
I gather each with smiles and tears
to know you're still around

Helping to assemble, too,
the broken bits of me
finding strength in collecting
each beloved memory

When your soul was freed and scattered
when mine set out to roam
I knew I'd keep on finding you
and always feel at home

Bloom Where You're Planted

Torn between: two places
two homes, two families, two lives
an unfamiliar, vast, empty shell
that I grew into
laid my foundations
to carefully construct
ma
propre
vie
each brick: a friend
a passion, a value, a desire
all building this marvellous, imperfect creation
that is mine
no directions, commands or inputs
a once intimidating autonomy
blossoming into the most beautiful flower:
unique and fragile and proud.

Will tearing it from its roots cause it to die?
Or can I merge these two lives and allow it to bloom
in a new home?

Many Homes

H: leave a piece of yourself

O: in each place you roam

M: create a collage of places

E: you get to call home

FORGET ME NOT

*

A flower of remembrance. So delicate and fragile.

Allowing us to see the beauty amongst our sadness.

Loss is inevitable but it can be lovely to connect with our sadness in a way

that makes us appreciate all of the wonderful things

we were lucky enough to have once had.

*

Forget-me-not

I don't want you
to forget me
even though
we are no longer
'us'

I want you
to remember
the times
we grew
together

* our fleeting moment in time *

with a smile
on your face
and warmth
in your heart

Goodbyes

Maybe, we struggle
so much with goodbyes
because suddenly we are
knocked down
by all of the gratitude
we forgot to express
the beautiful moments
we did not pay enough
attention to, take enough
mental pictures of
allow big enough smiles
or loud enough laughter
to erupt from
regret
of abusing the time
people and places
we were so lucky
to share these moments with

the fear of loss
never so real
questioning all of our actions
and decisions and promising NEVER
to take advantage
of such treasures again
Finally,
expressing our gratitude
and allowing our sadness
to take its course

Station Drop-off

A final wave goodbye
the unwavering loyalty of your loved ones
as they send you on your way
rain or shine
soaking in one last, precious embrace
longing it to last forever
tears of pride and sadness
deforming this priceless picture
as if being there
will convince you of their admiration
and maybe, just maybe
persuade you to stay

your image getting ever-smaller
as your final destination steals you away
yet, no matter how far you go
how small you've become
each time you turn around

they're still there.

Cheers

An *au revoir*
that tore my heart in two
a room filled with love, gratitude and tears
nostalgia flooding eyes
that aren't yet ready for this goodbye
how time flies

a silence, a look, a hug
a painted sunflower
to remember me by

friends, once strangers
finding new bonds
embracing the beauty
in our starkly different persons
backgrounds, journeys, paths
being brought together
one last time

To raise our glass:
a powerful cocktail
of friendship
and love
|
Santé

What Is Life Without Death

I'm very mindful
to be grateful
to not take for granted
the wonderful things in my life
but it feels impossible
to not become
complacent

fitting into mundane routines
wearing the tolls of daily life
Loud and Proud

it's not until
I start to sense my departure
that I shed this weight
and find light in my home again

maybe, it's the knowledge of
our inevitable departure
from this world
that sparks light upon
the rest of our lives

The Meaning Of Life

To continue inspiring
beyond your days

by a simple smile
and humble ways

puts silence to
our wandering minds

for all the meaning
we ache to find

You Are Alive

You are alive, each time
we hear your name
tell your stories
and sing your favourite songs

You are alive, each time
we repeat your kindness
practise your compassion
and show your understanding

You are alive, each time
we spread your joy
embody your smile
and share your love

You are

not

just

remembered

You are alive

Legacy

I am seeing with your eyes

exploring with your spirit

loving with your heart

you will always

live on

through me

Fading Away

You're treasured beyond your form, you see
when weak or frail
you're unchanged to me
so don't hide away, ashamed to be
the person I love
so dearly

Angel

I was angry
you did not let me
say goodbye

but now
I finally think
I understand why

you were always
planning to stay
close by

with all your new strength
that allows you
to fly

Life Goes On

I am sad to see life
keep moving

realising that it's possible
without you here

a harsh reality
that's painful to accept

but there's a subtle beauty in it, too

and I smile to think
that comes from you

Rain

The earth is crying
raining its tears
with such beauty
that cannot even begin
to replicate
what you gave it

or the true sadness
of its loss

Not Enough

How I cherish my memories
but they are not enough

my heart will forever ache
for the real thing

how I hate to tarnish
these precious moments

with the sadness of knowing
their fading remains

are all

I'll ever

have

Selfish Sadness

I am sad, not because
you are at peace
not because
you lived so many
wonderful, inspiring days
not because
you left
making sure we were armed
with the most precious memories
not because
you radiated such joy
and touched so many lives
in your allotted time

I am selfishly sad
for my loss
and the loss
of a more difficult
less magical world

Lay To Rest

I will find ways
to hug you
through the wind
to see your smile
through the sun
to hear your laugh
through the birds
to find your wisdom
through the stars

Rainbows And Clouds

I will look for you
in the rainbows and clouds
and even if others
cannot see your face
your warmth and laughter
will find me with grace

and there you'll be
present and living
through my smile

Curtain Call

Thank you for the moments
for the joy, for the love

Thank you for the wisdom
for the advice, for the hugs

For I would not exist as me
had you not played your key part

A show-stopping performance
an honest work of art

The applause keeps rolling loudly
your presence held around

Long after the stage is empty
long after
Your Final Bow.

PEACE LILY

*

A reminder to find peace amidst all of the beautiful chaos that consumes our lives.

Simple, calming and renewing. Helping to evoke a kindness and compassion

that is desperately needed in the world and in ourselves.

*

Peace Of Home

I found peace
on a Saturday afternoon, laying
on my stone garden floor
carefully centred
within a thin strip
of vanishing yellow light

soaking in
the last glow
of the day

The Best Way To Smile

To smile with your mouth
lifts the spirit

but to smile with your heart
warms the soul

A Friendly Reminder

When we remember
that we share
this world

and thrive only
when living
in harmony

we may just start
to take
more care

Whisked Away

A welcome warmly lit by fire
as my body marks the hour

swallowing the whole days load:
words, people, places,
troubles, smiles, laughter, tears, tasks,
nothing.

thoughts
…
in a race with the hand on the clock as I ask politely for their
ARRÊTE
and succumb, willingly
ready
to let sleep
wash over me
the waves
rhythmically nearing
eventually claiming
my ocean-bound body
to the vast depths
of wonder
darkness

f l o a t i n g

Beach Days

A soothing crash
of glistening wave
showering you
with the sweetest, salty air
paired with a sunshine glow
that gently warms your skin, shuts your eyes
and lifts the corners of your mouth
treading soft sands and pebbled waters
each: a treasure to someone
claimed
as their own
to bury deep within
their sea
of memories

Sunrise

Emerging colours
overwhelming the cool night sky
creating a miraculous display
of all the beauty, potential and wonder
in this brand-new day
…

Sunset

Black clouds bloodied red
as the sun washes its hands
clean of another day
displaying its work
in a momentary explosion
canvassing the sky
inspiring beauty in tomorrow.

Nature = Medicine

To wake before the world requires
just before
sunlight breaks

where the cold morning air gives a refreshing energy
and the birds sing you, gently, on your way

brings a peace that will soothe the soul
more than anything you could be prescribed

Natural Rhythm

Align with the rhythm of nature, allow
the birds to sing you softly
to rise
the sun to kiss you warmly
the skies
to reveal your true potential
as the imagination
flies
and fills your day with beauty
until the sun
decides
to paint the sky in shades of red
as we say our sweet
goodbyes.

Early Bird

Rise before

the rest of the world

bathe in the calm

bask in the beauty

breathe in

the sweet air

let it rinse

your mind

and carry you

through

the

day

To Grow With Grace

To grow old with wrinkles
to let our hair turn to silvery snow

to embrace the changes in our bodies
to keep our teeth-less smiles on show

to let our stories inspire
our experiences to humble
and memories to glow

is to grow
with grace

How I Want To Live

I aspire

to lead

my life

with kindness

and grace

to leave

behind me

a happier

place

You Are What You Breathe

There is so much kindness in this world.

Let us focus on that.

Let us breathe it in.

Let it become us.

My Legacy

My goal in this life
is to live as gently as possible
moving in rhythm
to the sweet dance
of the earth

flowing
with the tide
floating
beside the lily pads

allowing nature to guide
my wondrous adventure
of a life

close my eyes
follow the sun
complete trust

If my legacy
is to leave
this fragile beauty
untouched
with as minimal disturbance
as possible
I will be gentle
conscious
quiet
and mindful
and I hope
you will thank me
with your smile